French English
Picture Dictionary

Illustrated by Adam Pescott

BRIMAX

Contents

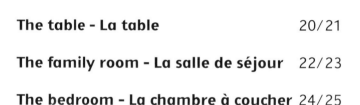

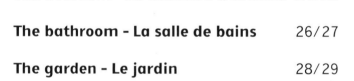

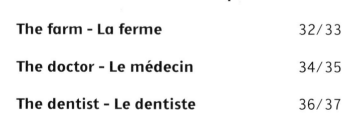

About this book

This picture dictionary presents familiar scenes and objects in a child's world. On each page, there are pictures labelled in French so that the child can practise saying the words. At the back of the book is a word list listing the French word, its pronunciation and its English translation.

To help make learning fun, most pages double as an "I Spy" activity. Where is the newspaper in the family room picture? Where is the worm in the garden picture? Children will enjoy looking for the objects that are pictured and named around the border of most pages.

Most of the words in this book are nouns (naming words). All French nouns are masculine or feminine. You can tell if a word is masculine or feminine by the little word that comes before the noun. **Le** is the word for "the" in front of a masculine noun and **la** is "the" in front of a feminine noun. For example, **le fermier** means "the farmer" and **la famille** means "the family." When a noun begins with a vowel sound (a,e,i,o,u) you put **l'** before the word instead of **le** or **la**. For example, **l'oncle** means "the uncle" and **l'arbre** means "the tree". We also do this before an "h" that is not pronounced. For example, **l'hôpital** means "the hospital."

In front of nouns that are plural (more than one object, such as "books") use **les** (the) before the word. We can use **les** in front of both masculine and feminine nouns. For example, "book" **le livre** becomes **les livres** when there is more than one and "woman" **la femme** becomes **les femmes**.

The family – **La famille**

father
le père

mother
la mère

grandfather
le grand-père

brother
le frère

sister
la sœur

baby
le bébé

uncle
l'oncle

aunt
la tante

grandmother
la grand-mère

female cousin
la cousine

male cousin
le cousin

The body
Le corps

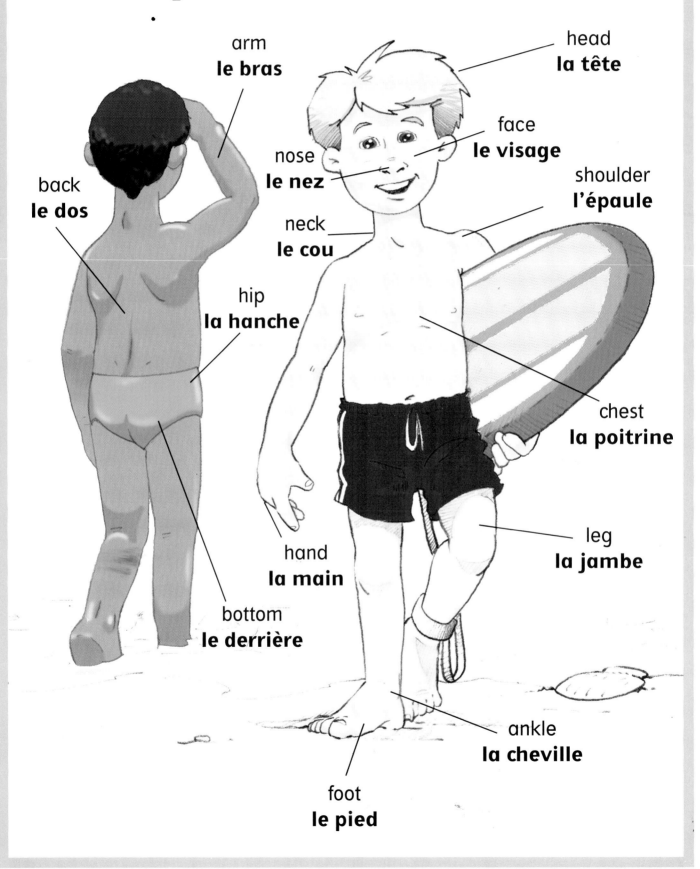

arm
le bras

head
la tête

face
le visage

nose
le nez

shoulder
l'épaule

back
le dos

neck
le cou

hip
la hanche

chest
la poitrine

hand
la main

leg
la jambe

bottom
le derrière

ankle
la cheville

foot
le pied

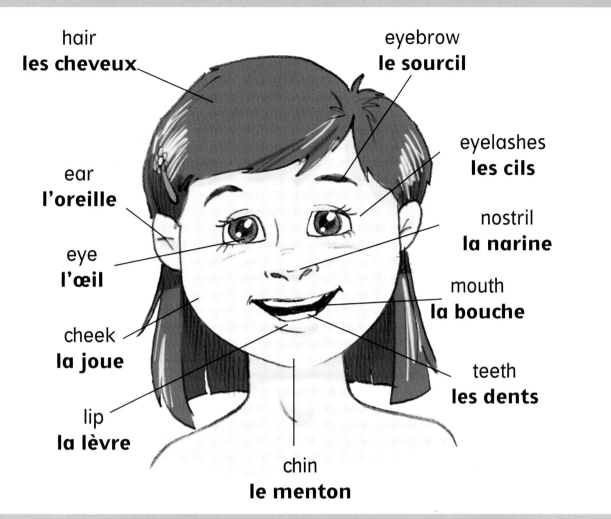

hair
les cheveux

eyebrow
le sourcil

eyelashes
les cils

ear
l'oreille

nostril
la narine

eye
l'œil

mouth
la bouche

cheek
la joue

teeth
les dents

lip
la lèvre

chin
le menton

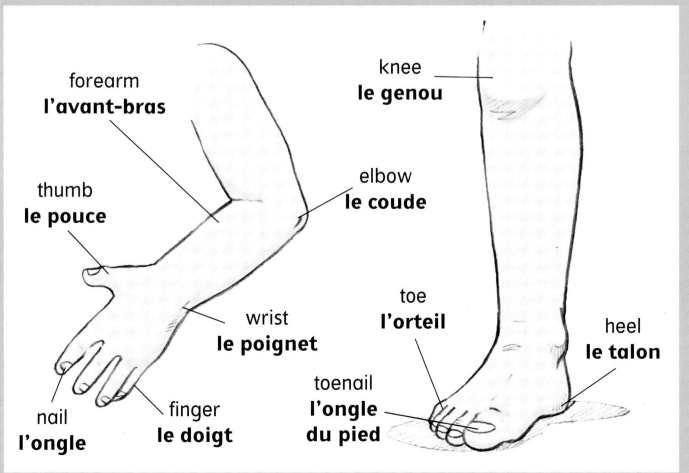

forearm
l'avant-bras

knee
le genou

thumb
le pouce

elbow
le coude

wrist
le poignet

toe
l'orteil

heel
le talon

nail
l'ongle

finger
le doigt

toenail
**l'ongle
du pied**

7

Colours – Les couleurs

brown
marron

black
noir

white
blanc

red
rouge

yellow
jaune

blue
bleu

blue **bleu** + yellow **jaune** = green **vert**

yellow **jaune** + red **rouge** = orange **orange**

red **rouge** + blue **bleu** = purple **violet**

Shapes – **Les formes**

square
le carré

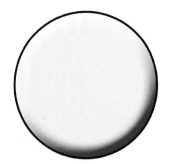

circle
le cercle

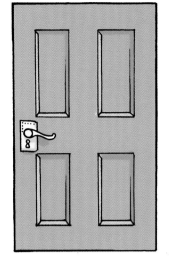

rectangle
le rectangle

diamond
le losange

triangle
le triangle

crescent
**le croissant
de lune**

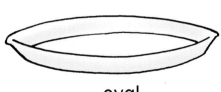

oval
l'ovale

star
l'étoile

heart
le cœur

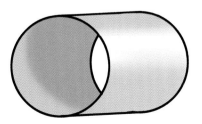

cylinder
le cylindre

cone
le cône

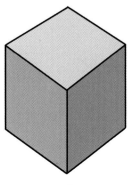

cube
le cube

Numbers
Les nombres

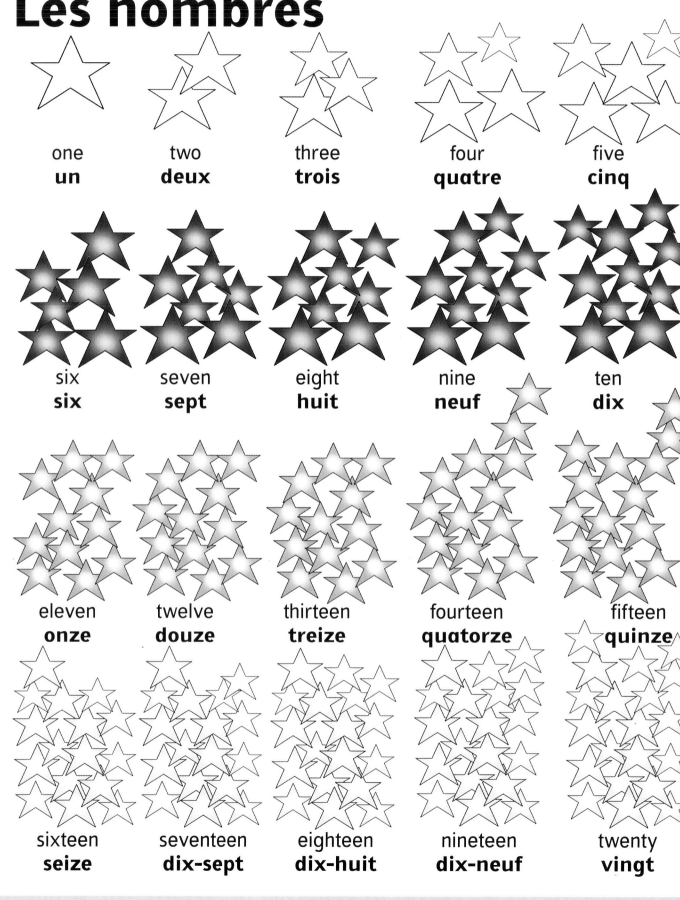

one **un**	two **deux**	three **trois**	four **quatre**	five **cinq**
six **six**	seven **sept**	eight **huit**	nine **neuf**	ten **dix**
eleven **onze**	twelve **douze**	thirteen **treize**	fourteen **quatorze**	fifteen **quinze**
sixteen **seize**	seventeen **dix-sept**	eighteen **dix-huit**	nineteen **dix-neuf**	twenty **vingt**

21
vingt et un
22
vingt-deux
23
vingt-trois

24
vingt-quatre
25
vingt-cinq
26
vingt-six

27
vingt-sept
28
vingt-huit
29
vingt-neuf

thirty
trente

forty
quarante

fifty
cinquante

sixty
soixante

seventy
soixante-dix

eighty
quatre-vingts

ninety
quatre-vingt-dix

hundred
cent

Mealtimes
Les heures du repas

milk
le lait

juice
le jus de fruits

Breakfast
Le petit déjeuner

yoghurt
le yaourt

cereal
les céréales

fruit
les fruits

honey
le miel

toast
le pain grillé

butter
le beurre

boiled eggs
les œufs à la coque

sausages
les saucisses

bacon
le bacon

Lunch
Le déjeuner

drink
la boisson

sandwich
le sandwich

pizza
la pizza

rolls
les petits pains

Dinner
Le dîner

MENU

Chicken
and Chips
**Le poulet rôti
avec les frites**

Apple Pie
**La tarte
aux pommes**

broccoli
les brocolis

cream
la crème

apple pie
**la tarte aux
pommes**

French fries
les frites

baked beans
les haricots

chicken
le poulet

Food
La nourriture

chicken
le poulet

pork chops
les côtes de porc

steak
le bifteck

tuna
le thon

fish
le poisson

fish fingers
les bâtonnets de poisson

bread
le pain

cheese
le fromage

eggs
les œufs

bagel
le bagel

croissant
le croissant

rice
le riz

pasta
les pâtes

biscuits
les biscuits

crisps
les chips

cakes
les petits-fours

sugar
le sucre

ice-cream
la glace

Drinks – **Les boissons**

milk
le lait

water
l'eau

milkshakes
les milk-shakes

juice
le jus de fruits

tea
le thé

coffee
le café

lemonade
la limonade

hot chocolate
le chocolat chaud

Fruit – **Les fruits**

oranges
les oranges

apples
les pommes

pears
les poires

peaches
les pêches

lemons
les citrons

bananas
les bananes

melon
le melon

blueberries
les myrtilles

pineapple
l'ananas

strawberries
les fraises

grapes
les raisins

tomatoes
les tomates

Vegetables – **Les légumes**

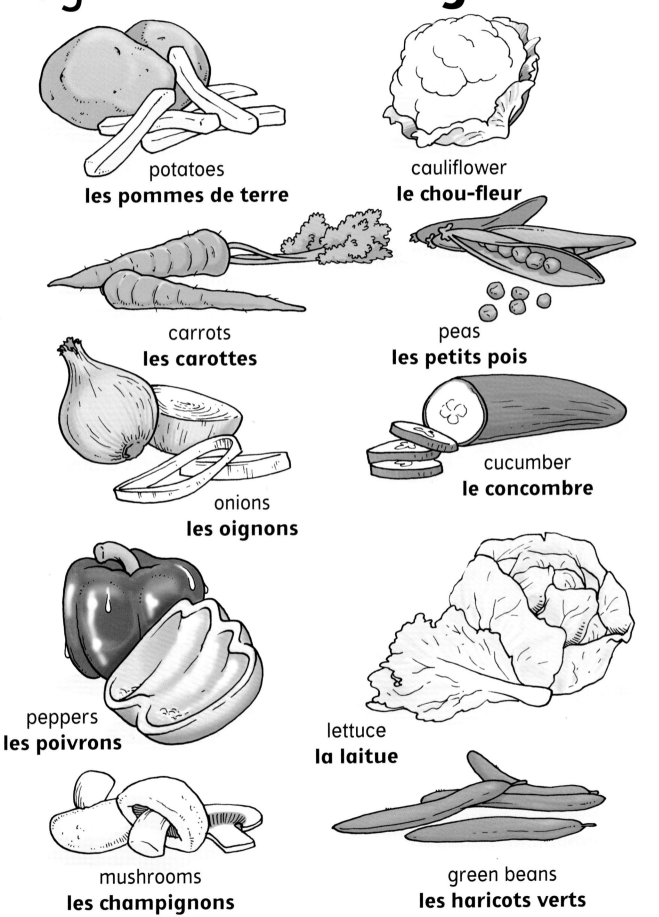

potatoes
les pommes de terre

cauliflower
le chou-fleur

carrots
les carottes

peas
les petits pois

onions
les oignons

cucumber
le concombre

peppers
les poivrons

lettuce
la laitue

mushrooms
les champignons

green beans
les haricots verts

The kitchen

apron
le tablier

mixing bowl
le bol

clock
l'horloge

wooden spoon
la cuillère en bois

dishwasher
le lave-vaisselle

whisk
le fouet

butter
le beurre

kitchen knife
le couteau de cuisine

La cuisine

sink
l'évier

toaster
le grille-pain

chair
la chaise

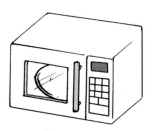

microwave
le micro-ondes

stove
la cuisinière

cutting board
la planche à pain

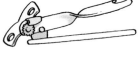

can opener
l'ouvre-boîte

mug
la grande tasse

The table

jug
le pichet

plate
l'assiette

casserole dish
la marmite

soup spoon
la cuillère à soupe

soup bowl
l'assiette creuse

knife
le couteau

butter dish
le beurrier

La table

salt
le sel
pepper
le poivre

napkin
la serviette

teaspoon
la cuillère à café

cup and saucer
**la tasse et
la soucoupe**

glass
le verre

side plate
la petite assiette

fork
la fourchette

spoon
la cuillère

The family room

stool
le tabouret

plant
la plante

armchair
le fauteuil

fireplace
la cheminée

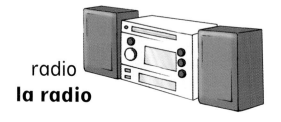

radio
la radio

newspaper
le journal

La salle de séjour

sofa
le canapé

vase
le vase

picture
le tableau

television
la télévision

window
la fenêtre

curtains
les rideaux

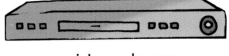

magazine
le magazine

video player
le magnétoscope

23

The bedroom

slippers
les pantoufles

baseball cap
**la casquette
de base-ball**

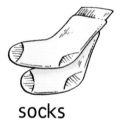

socks
les chaussettes

trainers
les tennis

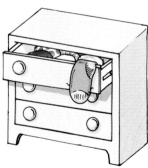

chest of drawers
la commode

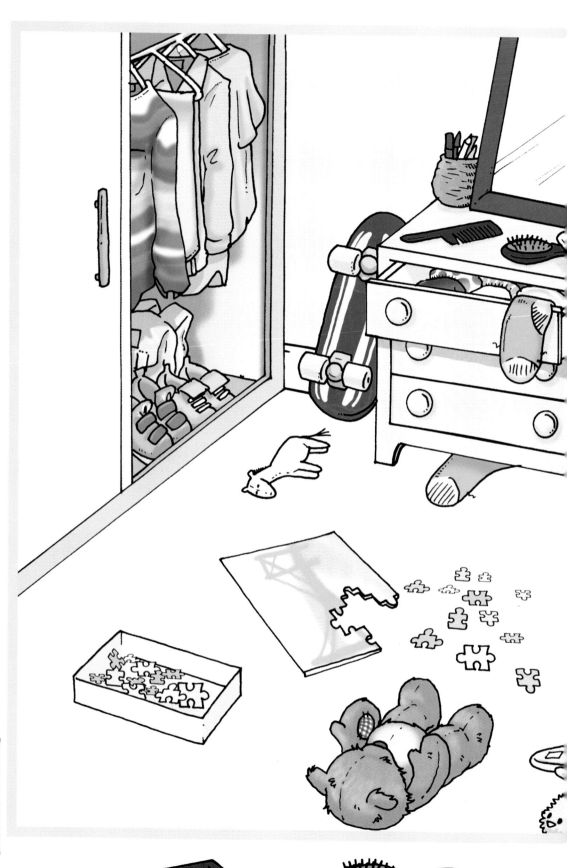

comb
le peigne

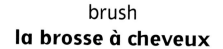

brush
la brosse à cheveux

La chambre à coucher

jeans
le jean

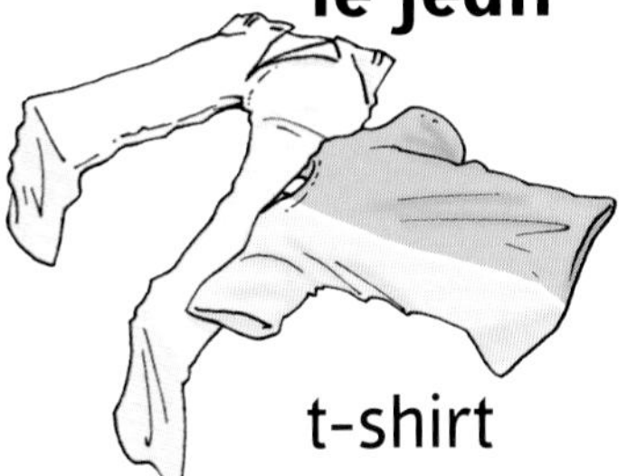

t-shirt
le tee-shirt

lamp
la lampe

mirror
le miroir

teddy bear
l'ours en peluche

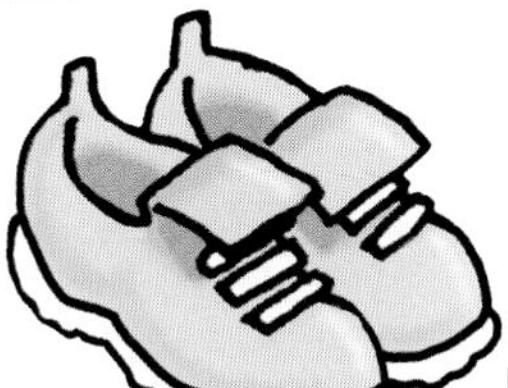

shoes
les chaussures

jigsaw puzzle
le puzzle

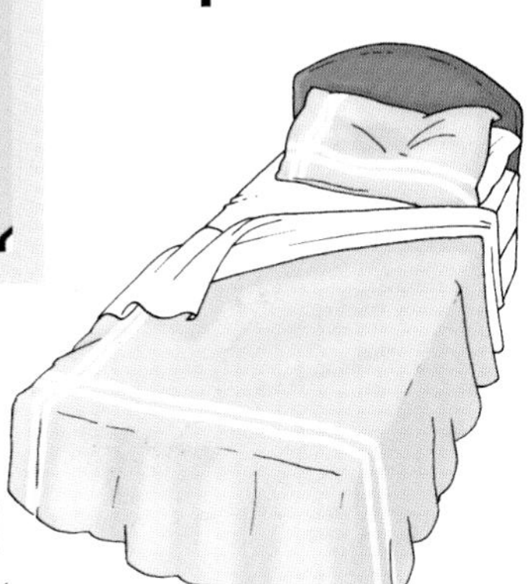

bed
le lit

The bathroom

toilet
les toilettes

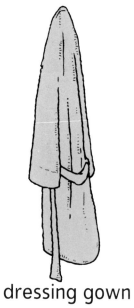

dressing gown
la robe de chambre

sink
le lavabo

shelf
l'étagère

shower
la douche

rubber duck
le canard de bain

soap
le savon

La salle de bains

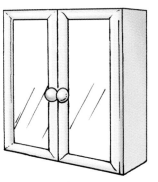

mirror
le miroir

bubble bath
le bain moussant

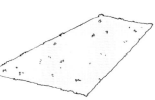

bathmat
le tapis de bain

towels
les serviettes

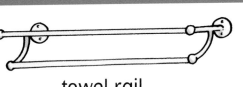

towel rail
le porte-serviettes

shampoo
le shampooing

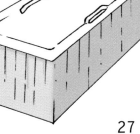

bath
la baignoire

The garden

tree
l'arbre

flowerpots
**les pots
de fleurs**

watering can
l'arrosoir

shed
**l'abri de
jardin**

bush
l'arbuste

snail
l'escargot

Le jardin

hose
le tuyau

shovel
la pelle

flowers
les fleurs

birds
les oiseaux

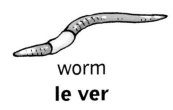

worm
le ver

butterfly
le papillon

wheelbarrow
la brouette

Pets
Les animaux domestiques

kittens
les chatons

cat
le chat

dog
le chien

puppies
les chiots

goldfish
le poisson rouge

tortoise
la tortue

guinea pig
le cochon d'Inde

hamster
le hamster

mice
les souris

budgerigar
la perruche

parrot
le perroquet

canaries
les canaris

rabbits
les lapins

The farm

farmer
le fermier

cow
la vache

calf
le veau

bull
le taureau

gate
la barrière

cockerel
le coq

chick
le poussin

La ferme

tractor
le tracteur

goat
la chèvre

pig
le cochon

sheep
le mouton

goose
l'oie

hen
la poule

hay
le foin

duck
le canard

33

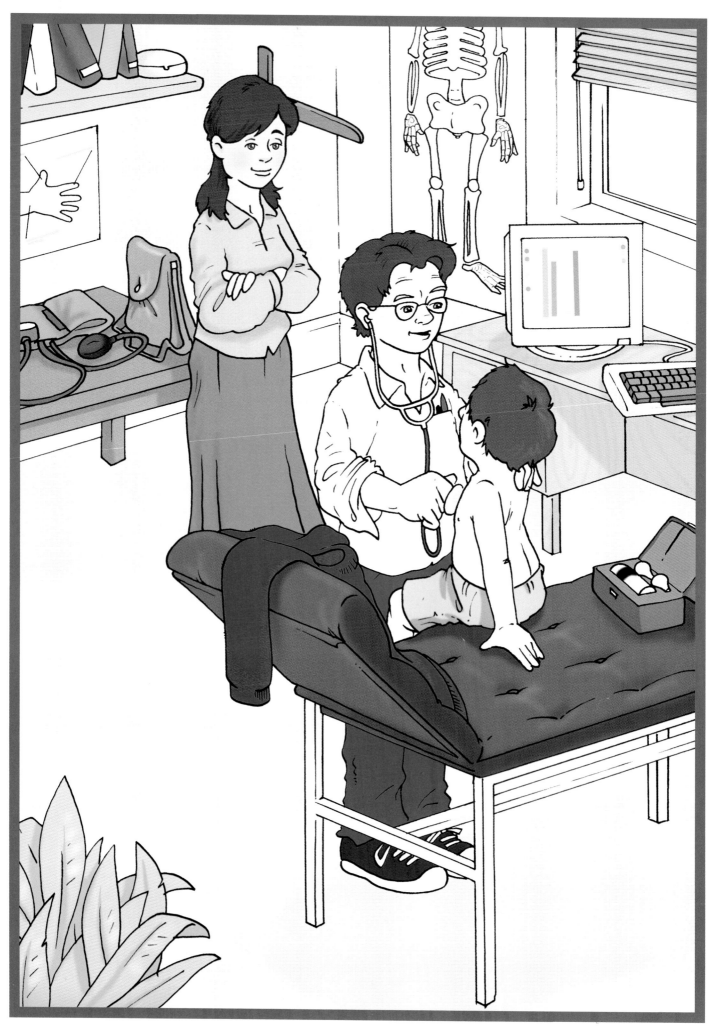

The doctor – **Le médecin**

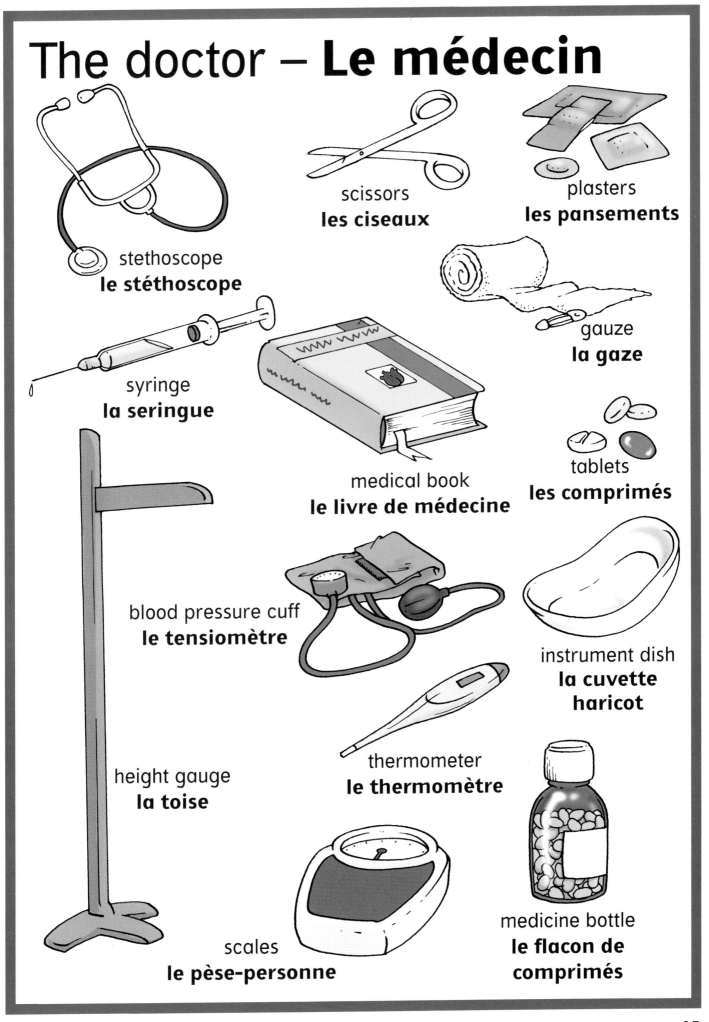

stethoscope
le stéthoscope

scissors
les ciseaux

plasters
les pansements

syringe
la seringue

gauze
la gaze

medical book
le livre de médecine

tablets
les comprimés

blood pressure cuff
le tensiomètre

instrument dish
la cuvette haricot

height gauge
la toise

thermometer
le thermomètre

scales
le pèse-personne

medicine bottle
le flacon de comprimés

The dentist – **Le dentiste**

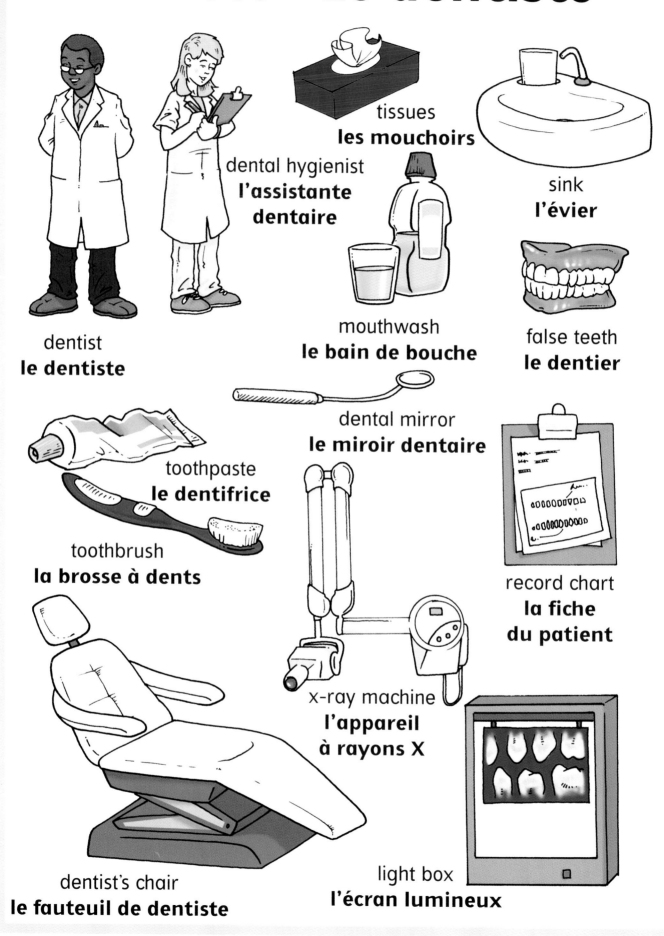

tissues
les mouchoirs

sink
l'évier

dental hygienist
l'assistante dentaire

dentist
le dentiste

mouthwash
le bain de bouche

false teeth
le dentier

dental mirror
le miroir dentaire

toothpaste
le dentifrice

toothbrush
la brosse à dents

record chart
la fiche du patient

x-ray machine
l'appareil à rayons X

dentist's chair
le fauteuil de dentiste

light box
l'écran lumineux

The classroom

teacher
l'institutrice

paper
le papier

globe
le globe

exercise book
le cahier

backpack
le sac à dos

Aa Bb Cc Dd Ee
Ff Gg Hh Ii Jj
Kk Ll Mm Nn Oo
Pp Qq Rr Ss Tt
Uu Vv Ww Xx Yy Zz

pencils
les crayons

ruler
la règle

pencil sharpener
le taille-crayon

Le salle de classe

computer
l'ordinateur

desk
le pupitre

glue
la colle

pencil case
**la trousse
à crayons**

crayons
**les crayons de
couleur**

scissors
les ciseaux

paintbrushes
les pinceaux

eraser
la gomme

box of paints
**la boîte de
peinture**

Sports
Les sports

basketball
le basket

baseball
le base-ball

soccer
le football

horse riding
l'équitation

running
la course

ice skating
le patinage

swimming
la natation

gymnastics
la gymnastique

judo
le judo

snowboarding
le snowboard

tennis
le tennis

cycling
le cyclisme

skiing
le ski

golf
le golf

American football
le football américain

Word list

This is a list of all the French words in this book, arranged in alphabetical order, followed by the word in English.

Tips for saying the words correctly. The following are some letters that are pronounced differently in French. Here's how to say them:

c and **qu** as in the "**k**" in the English word "**kite**"

ch as in the "**sh**" in the English word "**shop**"

g as in the "**g**" in the English word "**goat**"

g (before an e or i) and **j**, as in the "**s**" in the English word "**pleasure**"

h in many words is not sounded

th as in the "**t**" in the English word "**total**"

A

l'abri de jardin	labri duh jardan	shed
l'ananas	lanana	pineapple
les animaux domestiques	lay zanimow domessteek	pets
l'appareil à rayons X	laparay a rayon eeks	x-ray machine
l'arbre	larbr	tree
l'arbuste	larboost	bush
l'arrosoir	larroswhar	watering can
l'assiette	lass-yet	plate
l'assiette creuse	lass-yet kruhz	soup bowl
l'assistante dentaire	lassesstant dontair	dental hygienist
l'avant-bras	lavan-brah	forearm

B

le bacon	luh baycon	bacon
le bagel	luh bagel	bagel
la baignoire	la ban-nwahr	bath
le bain de bouche	luh ban duh boosh	mouthwash
le bain moussant	luh ban moosson	bubble bath
les bananes	lay banan	bananas
la barrière	lah baree-air	gate
le base-ball	luh base-ball	baseball
le basket	luh basket	basketball
les bâtonnets de poisson	lay batoneh duh pwasson	fish fingers
le bébé	luh bay-bay	baby
le beurre	luh burr	butter
le beurrier	luh burryer	butter dish
le bifteck	luh bifteck	steak
les biscuits	lay beeskwee	biscuits
blanc	blon	white
bleu	blur	blue
les boissons	lay bwasson	drinks
la boîte de peinture	la bwat duh pantoor	box of paints
le bol	luh boll	mixing bowl
la bouche	lah boosh	mouth

le bras	luh brah	arm
les brocolis	lay brokolee	broccoli
la brosse à dents	lah bross a don	toothbrush
la brosse à cheveux	lah bross a shuhvuh	brush
la brouette	lah broo-et	wheelbarrow
C		
le café	luh kafay	coffee
le cahier	luh ky-yay	exercise book
le canapé	luh kanapay	sofa
le canard	luh kanar	duck
le canard de bain	luh kanar duh ban	rubber duck
les canaris	lay kanaree	canaries
les carottes	lay karrot	carrots
le carré	luh karray	square
la casquette de base-ball	la kasket duh base-ball	baseball cap
cent	son	hundred
le cercle	luh sercle	circle
les céréales	lay sayrayahl	cereal
la chaise	lah shez	chair
la chambre à coucher	lah shonbr a kooshay	bedroom
les champignons	lay shonpeen-yon	mushrooms
le chat	luh sha	cat
les chatons	lay shaton	kittens
les chaussettes	lay sho-set	socks
les chaussures	lay sho-soor	shoes
la cheminée	lah sheminay	fireplace
les cheveux	lay shervur	hair
la cheville	lah sherveey	ankle
la chèvre	lah shevr	goat
le chien	luh shee-an	dog
les chiots	lay shee-ot	puppies
les chips	lay sheepss	crisps
le chocolat chaud	luh shokkollah sho	hot chocolate
le chou-fleur	luh shoo flurr	cauliflower
les cils	lay see	eyelashes
cinq	sank	five
cinquante	sank-ont	fifty
les ciseaux	lay seezo	scissors
les citrons	lay see-tron	lemons
le cochon	luh koshon	pig
le cochon d'Inde	luh koshon dande	guinea pig
le cœur	luh kurr	heart
la colle	lah koll	glue
la commode	lah kommode	chest of drawers
les comprimés	lay kom-pree-may	tablets
le concombre	luh kawnkawnbr	cucumber
le cône	luh kon	cone
le coq	luh kok	cockerel
le corps	luh kor	body
les côtes de porc	lay koht duh por	pork chops
le cou	luh koo	neck
le coude	luh kood	elbow
les couleurs	lay koolurr	colours
la course	lah koorss	running
le cousin	luh kouzan	male cousin
la cousine	lah koozeen	female cousin
le couteau	luh kooto	knife
le couteau de cuisine	luh kooto duh kwizeen	kitchen knife

les crayons	lay kray-on	pencils
les crayons de couleur	lay kray-on duh koolurr	crayons
la crème	lah krehm	cream
le croissant	luh krwasson	croissant
le croissant de lune	luh krwasson duh loon	crescent
le cube	luh koob	cube
la cuillère	lah kwee-yair	spoon
la cuillère à café	lah kwee-yair a kafay	teaspoon
la cuillère à soupe	lah kwee-yair a soop	soup spoon
la cuillère en bois	lah kwee-yair on bwa	wooden spoon
la cuisine	lah kweezeen	kitchen
la cuisinière	lah kweezeen-yair	stove
la cuvette haricot	lah koo-vet-areeko	instrument dish
le cyclisme	luh seekleess-muh	cycling
le cylindre	luh silandr	cylinder
D		
le déjeuner	luh day-junay	lunch
le dentier	luh dont-yay	false teeth
le dentifrice	luh dont-ee-freess	toothpaste
le dentiste	luh donteest	dentist
les dents	lay don	teeth
le derrière	luh dairyair	bottom
deux	duh	two
le dîner	luh deenay	dinner
dix	deess	ten
dix-huit	deess weet	eighteen
dix-neuf	deess nuf	nineteen
dix-sept	deess seht	seventeen
le doigt	luh dwah	finger
le dos	luh doh	back
la douche	lah doosh	shower
douze	dooz	twelve
E		
l'eau	lo	water
l'écran lumineux	lay kran loomeenuh	light box
l'épaule	laypol	shoulder
l'équitation	laykeetass-yon	horse riding
l'escargot	leskargo	snail
l'étoile	laytwal	star
l'étagère	laytajair	shelf
l'évier	layv-yay	sink (kitchen)
F		
la famille	lah famee	family
le fauteuil	luh fotuh-ee	armchair
le fauteuil de dentiste	luh fotuh-ee duh donteest	dentist's chair
la fenêtre	lah fuhnetr	window
la ferme	lah fairm	farm
le fermier	luh fairm-yay	farmer
la fiche du patient	lah feesh dew pashon	record chart
le flacon de comprimés	luh flakon duh kom-preemay	medicine bottle
les fleurs	lay flurr	flowers
le foin	luh fwan	hay
le football	luh football	soccer
le football américain	luh football amairican	American football
les formes	lay form	shapes
le fouet	luh fweh	whisk
la fourchette	lah foorshet	fork

French	Pronunciation	English
les fraises	lay frez	strawberries
les frites	lay freet	French fries
le frère	luh frair	brother
le fromage	luh fromahj	cheese
les fruits	lay frwee	fruit
G		
la gaze	lah gaz	gauze
le genou	luh juh-noo	knee
la glace	lah glahss	ice-cream
le globe	luh globb	globe
le golf	luh golf	golf
la gomme	lah gom	eraser
la grand–mère	lah gron mair	grandmother
le grand-père	luh gron pair	grandfather
la grande tasse	lah grond tass	mug
le grille-pain	luh gree-pan	toaster
la gymnastique	lah jeemnasteek	gymnastics
H		
le hamster	luh amstair	hamster
la hanche	lahonsh	hip
les haricots	lay zareeko	baked beans
les haricots verts	lay zareeko ver	green beans
les heures du repas	lay zurr dew ruhpa	mealtimes
l'horloge	lorloj	clock
huit	weet	eight
I		
l'institutrice	lansteetutreece	teacher
J		
la jambe	lah jonb	leg
le jardin	luh jardan	garden
jaune	jo-n	yellow
le jean	luh jean	jeans
la joue	lah joo	cheek
le journal	luh joornal	newspaper
le judo	luh joodo	judo
le jus de fruits	luh joo duh frwee	juice
L		
le lait	luh lay	milk
la laitue	lah laytew	lettuce
la lampe	lah lonp	lamp
les lapins	lay lapan	rabbits
le lavabo	luh la-va-bo	sink (bathroom)
le lave-vaisselle	luh lav-vess-el	dishwasher
les légumes	lay laygoom	vegtables
la lèvre	lah lehvr	lip
la limonade	lah leemonahd	lemonade
le lit	luh lee	bed
le livre de médecine	luh leevr duh maydseen	medical book
le losange	luh lozanj	diamond
M		
le magazine	luh magazeen	magazine
le magnétoscope	luh manyaytoskop	video player
la main	lah man	hand
la marmite	lah marmeet	casserole dish
marron	maron	brown
le médecin	luh maydsan	doctor

le melon	luh muhlon	melon
le menton	luh monton	chin
la mère	lah mair	mother
le micro-ondes	luh meecro-ond	microwave
le miel	luh mee-el	honey
les milk-shakes	lay milk-shake	milkshakes
le miroir	luh meerwahr	mirror
le miroir dentaire	luh meer-wahr dontair	dental mirror
les mouchoirs	lay mooshwahr	tissues
le mouton	luh mooton	sheep
les myrtilles	lay meerteye	blueberries
N		
la narine	lah nareen	nostril
la natation	lah natass-yon	swimming
neuf	nuf	nine
le nez	luh nay	nose
noir	nwahr	black
les nombres	lay nombre	numbers
la nourriture	lah nooreetoor	food
O		
l'œil	luh-ee	eye
les œufs	lay zuh	eggs
les œufs à la coque	lay zuh ah lah kok	boiled eggs
l'oie	lwah	goose
les oignons	lay zon-yon	onions
les oiseaux	lay zwazo	birds
l'oncle	lonkl	uncle
l'ongle	longl	nail
l'ongle du pied	longl doo p-yay	toenail
onze	onz	eleven
orange	oronj	orange
les oranges	lay zoronj	oranges
l'ordinateur	lordeenaturr	computer
l'oreille	loray	ear
l'orteil	lortay	toe
l'ours en peluche	loor zon puhloosh	teddy bear
l'ouvre-boîte	loovr-bwat	can opener
l'ovale	lovvahl	oval
P		
le pain	luh pan	bread
le pain grillé	luh pan greeyay	toast
les pansements	lay ponssmon	plasters
les pantoufles	lay pontoofl	slippers
le papier	luh pap-yay	paper
le papillon	luh papee-yon	butterfly
les pâtes	lay pat	pasta
le patinage	luh pateenaj	ice skating
les pêches	lay pehsh	peaches
le peigne	luh pehn	comb
la pelle	lah pel	shovel
le père	luh pair	father
le perroquet	luh perrokeh	parrot
la perruche	lah perroosh	budgerigar
le pèse-personne	luh pess-person	scales
le petit déjeuner	luh puhtee dayjuhnay	breakfast
la petite assiette	lah puhtee ass-yet	side plate
les petits-fours	lay puhtee foor	cakes

French	Pronunciation	English
les petits pains	lay puhtee pan	rolls
les petits pois	lay puhtee pwa	peas
le pichet	luh peeshay	jug
le pied	luh p-yay	foot
les pinceaux	lay panso	paintbrushes
la pizza	lah pizza	pizza
la planche à pain	lah plonsh a pan	cutting board
la plante	lah plont	plant
le poignet	luh pwan-yay	wrist
les poires	lay pwahr	pears
le poisson	luh pwasson	fish
le poisson rouge	luh pwasson rooj	goldfish
la poitrine	lah pwahtreen	chest
le poivre	luh pwahvr	pepper
les poivrons	lay pwahvron	peppers
les pommes	lay pom	apples
les pommes de terre	lay pom duh tair	potatoes
le porte-serviettes	luh port-sairvee-et	towel rail
les pots de fleurs	lay pot duh flurr	flowerpots
le pouce	luh pooss	thumb
la poule	lah pool	hen
le poulet	luh pooleh	chicken
le poussin	luh poossan	chick
le pupitre	luh pew-peetr	desk
le puzzle	luh poosl	puzzle
Q		
quarante	karont	forty
quatorze	katorz	fourteen
quatre	katr	four
quatre-vingts	katr-van	eighty
quatre-vingt-dix	katr-van-deess	ninety
quinze	kanz	fifteen
R		
la radio	lah ra-deeo	radio
les raisins	lay rezzan	grapes
le rectangle	luh rektangl	rectangle
la règle	lah rehgl	ruler
les rideaux	lay reedo	curtains
le riz	luh ree	rice
la robe de chambre	lah rob duh shonbr	dressing gown
rouge	rooj	red
S		
le sac à dos	luh sak a doh	backpack
la salle de bains	lah sal duh ban	bathroom
la salle de classe	lah sal duh klass	classroom
la salle de séjour	lah sal duh sayjoor	family room
le sandwich	luh sondweetch	sandwich
les saucisses	lay soasseess	sausages
le savon	luh savon	soap
seize	sehz	sixteen
le sel	luh sel	salt
sept	set	seven
la seringue	lah sair-ang	syringe
la serviette	lah sairvee-et	napkin
les serviettes	lay sairvee-et	towels
le shampooing	luh shonpwan	shampoo
six	seess	six

le ski	luh skee	skiing
le snowboard	luh snowboard	snowboarding
la sœur	lah surr	sister
soixante	swassont	sixty
soixante-dix	swassont dees	seventy
le sourcil	luh soorseel	eyebrow
les souris	lay soor-ee	mice
les sports	lay spor	sports
le stéthoscope	luh stet-o-skop	stethoscope
le sucre	luh sookr	sugar
T		
la table	lah tahbl	table
le tableau	luh tablo	picture
le tablier	luh tablyay	apron
le tabouret	luh tabooray	stool
le taille-crayon	luh ty-crayon	pencil sharpener
le talon	luh talon	heel
la tante	lah tont	aunt
le tapis de bain	luh tapee duh ban	bathmat
la tarte aux pommes	lah tart o pom	apple pie
la tasse et la soucoupe	lah tass ay lah sookoop	cup and saucer
le taureau	luh toro	bull
le tee-shirt	luh teeshirt	t-shirt
la télévision	lah taylayveez-yon	television
le tennis	luh tenneess	tennis
les tennis	lay tenneess	trainers
le tensiomètre	luh tonsyo-metr	blood pressure cuff
la tête	lah tet	head
le thé	luh tay	tea
le thermomètre	luh tairmometr	thermometer
le thon	luh ton	tuna
les toilettes	lay twalet	toilet
la toise	lah twaz	height gauge
les tomates	lay tommaht	tomatoes
la tortue	lah tortoo	tortoise
le tracteur	luh trak-turr	tractor
treize	trehz	thirteen
trente	tront	thirty
le triangle	luh treeongl	triangle
trois	trwah	three
la trousse à crayons	lah trooss ah kray-on	pencil case
le tuyau	luh twee-yo	hose
U		
un	an	one
V		
la vache	lah vash	cow
le vase	luh vahz	vase
le veau	luh vo	calf
le ver	luh vair	worm
le verre	luh vair	glass
vert	vair	green
vingt	van	twenty
violet	veeolay	purple
le visage	luh veezahj	face
Y		
le yaourt	luh ya-oort	yoghurt